This book belongs to

_____

A BOY'S GUIDE TO PRAYER

JIM GEORGE

HARVEST HOUSE PUBLISHERS
EUGENE, OREGON

Cover design by Garborg Design Works

Cover photos © Aletia / BIGSTOCK

HARVEST KIDS is a trademark of The Hawkins Children's LLC. Harvest House Publishers, Inc., is the exclusive licensee of the trademark HARVEST KIDS.

A Boy's Guide to Prayer
Copyright © by 2019 Jim George
Published by Harvest House Publishers
Eugene, Oregon 97408
www.harvesthousepublishers.com

ISBN 978-0-7369-7554-4 (pbk.)
ISBN 978-0-7369-7555-1 (eBook)

Printed in the United States of America

19 20 21 22 23 24 25 26 / VP-CD / 10 9 8 7 6 5 4 3 2 1

To my courageous grandson, Ryan—

Trust in the Lord with all your heart,
and lean on Him
for strength and guidance
all the days of your life.

(Proverbs 3:5-6)

Contents

When I was a young boy about your age, my dad made a deal with me. He said he would replace any money I put into a savings account. That meant for every dollar I took to the bank, my dad would give me a dollar. I couldn't believe it! What a deal! Little did I know that my dad was teaching me the habit of saving money. And guess what? Even to this day I still practice the habit of saving money.

Now you might ask, "What does saving money have to do with learning how to pray?" Well, it's the same principle: Like learning to save money, learning to pray is a habit that will help you through your entire life.

Have you heard of muscle memory? It's the result of doing something over and over again. Eventually, you don't even have to think about it—your muscles automatically perform that task, like kicking a soccer ball or hitting a baseball. But in this book, we are going to be developing "spiritual" muscle memory when it comes to prayer.

Most great athletes or musicians begin developing their skills at an early age. If you can learn the importance of prayer now, you can develop the habit of prayer and be well on your way to growing into a man after God's own heart.

But don't start this journey alone. Ask your best friend to join you in this adventure of learning to pray. Or maybe you and the boys' class at church could go through this book together. Or maybe one of your parents could work through this book with you. Who knows? Maybe they, too, could get excited about praying!

God is looking for young men who will be like King David. God said, "He will do everything I want him to do" (Acts 13:22)—and prayer will help you be that kind of man. If you want be a young man after God's own heart, the future begins today as you start your journey of learning more about prayer by reading *A Boy's Guide to Prayer.* Enjoy the journey!

Your friend and fellow prayer warrior,

Jim George

1

Talking Things
Over with God

Have you ever noticed a guy who looks like he's talking to himself? You might even do this too. Well, when you talk to yourself, it's only a one-way conversation. You are just saying what you are thinking in your mind and your heart.

But when you *pray* and talk to *God*, that's a totally different story!

So, what is prayer?

Prayer Is an Act of Faith

If you have tried to pray, you probably agree with me that prayer can be difficult and feel awkward. Why is that?

One reason is that you can't see or touch the one you are praying to.

Another reason is that you can't and won't hear any response to your prayers. It seems like you are just talking to the air. So there you are, doing what appears to you or others to be talking to yourself.

But is that really true? If you want to make sure you are not just talking to yourself, but you are really talking to God—to Someone who can actually hear you and help you with your problems and needs—there is a verse that will help you. Here's what it says:

> *Anyone who wants to come to him must believe that God exists and that he rewards those who sincerely seek him* (Hebrews 11:6).

What does this verse say is the first thing you must do if you want God to hear your prayers?

"Anyone who wants to come to him [God]

must _____ that God

_____..."

To believe means to have faith. It means you are confident that even though you cannot see God, He is real—He does exist.

This verse goes on to explain how prayer and faith work together.

"Anyone who wants to come to him [God] must believe

that God exists and that he _____

those who sincerely seek him."

If you have faith that God exists, you can and are to sincerely seek Him. "Sincerely" means to be honest, truthful, genuine, and straightforward.

Prayer Should Be Ongoing

When you talk to your parents and friends, you probably don't stop with a simple "hello." No, you keep on talking and discussing all kinds of guy things with that person.

The same is true about prayer. Prayer is not a one-time talk or a simple greeting or request for something. No, prayer is meant to be an ongoing discussion with God. You can talk with God about anything, at any time, for as long as you want, and as often as you want. Here's how Jesus described the process of ongoing prayer:

> *Keep on asking, and you will receive what you ask for. Keep on seeking, and you will find. Keep on knocking, and the door will be opened to you* (Matthew 7:7).

In your own words, when God tells you to "keep on" doing something, what does it mean you should do when it comes to prayer?

_____

_____

_____

_____

God knows you, loves you, and wants to hear from you. One way you can let Him know you love Him is to keep on praying and asking Him for His help about everything in your life. Matthew 6:8 explains how this works:

For everyone who asks, receives. Everyone who seeks, finds. And to everyone who knocks, the door will be opened.

Jesus gives you a word picture to describe how God answers your prayers.

"And to everyone who knocks, the _____

will _____ _____."

First Thessalonians 5:17 says:

Never stop praying.

According to this verse, how often should you pray?

_____

Philippians 4:6 tells you what to do instead of worrying. Read the verse below and *circle* what you should not do. Then *underline* what you should do instead.

Don't worry about anything; instead, pray about everything.

Jesus Shows You the Way to Pray

Prayers spoken in faith are real and meaningful, and they produce results. Everyone will tell you prayer is a blessing. But sometimes it's hard to remember to pray. Maybe that's because we are so busy.

Or maybe it's because we have so many fun things to do, so many activities to enjoy, and so many friends to enjoy, we forget about praying.

And sometimes we don't pray because deep down inside, we don't believe prayer matters. We don't believe it really makes a difference. We aren't 100 percent sure God hears our prayers.

Whatever the reason, most people—kids, adults, and even your pastor!—don't pray as often or as sincerely as they want to or should.

> If you are not happy with your prayer life, or
>
> if you are just getting started, or
>
> if you are just beginning to understand prayer, or
>
> if you want more results from praying,

then learning more about Jesus and His habit of prayer will be helpful.

First, understand that Jesus was and is God—God the Son. Because He was God, Jesus didn't need to pray. He already knew all things in the past, the present, and the future. Yet when Jesus came to earth, He chose to be the perfect model for us, to show us how we should live our lives and depend on God. Because of His choice, He shows us how to pray.

Jesus lived in an attitude of prayer. His mind was always focused upward, toward God. No matter where He was or what was happening around Him or to Him, Jesus prayed. Prayer was Jesus' life, His habit, and His link to God the Father. He talked everything over with His Father in heaven. Nothing was too small to pray about. For instance...

Jesus prayed before making decisions. Read Luke 6:12-13 below.

One day soon afterward Jesus went up on a mountain to pray, and he prayed to God all night. At daybreak he called together all of his disciples and chose twelve of them to be apostles.

What key decision did Jesus make after praying?

_____

_____

And how long did Jesus pray before making this decision?

_____

_____

What do you need to do as you tackle the decisions you need to make, both big and small?

_____

_____

_____

_____

_____

Jesus prayed for others. Praying for others was a pattern for Jesus during His time on earth. For instance, on the night before His death, Jesus told His disciples—and specifically, Peter—that the devil had asked permission to test the disciples with a severe trial. Jesus said to Peter, who was also called Simon,

Simon, Simon, Satan has asked to sift each of you like wheat (Luke 22:31).

After Jesus gave this warning, He added this:

But I have pleaded in prayer for you, Simon, that your faith should not fail (Luke 22:32).

What did Jesus do for Peter that would comfort him?

"...I have _____ in

_____ for _____..."

Jesus prayed for others, and so should you. Who are the people you can pray for today? List a few names and begin to pray for them—maybe even right this minute. Then set up a regular time to pray for them. And be sure to start with your parents and brothers and sisters!

_____

_____

_____

Jesus Gives You a Model Prayer

Just like you and me, Jesus' disciples seemed to need help with praying. Wisely, they asked Jesus, "Lord, teach us to pray..." (Luke 11:1). Jesus then gave them—and us—a model or sample prayer to pray. This prayer is usually referred to as the Lord's Prayer. Read it now in the verses below. Then answer the questions that guide you through an outline of the contents of this famous prayer. It's in Matthew 6:9-13. Jesus began by saying, "Pray like this:"

⁹ *Our Father in heaven, Your name is holy.*

¹⁰ *May Your holy nation come. What You want done, may it be done on earth as it is in heaven.*

¹¹ *Give us the bread we need today.*

¹² *Forgive us our sins as we forgive those who sin against us.*

¹³ *Do not let us be tempted, but keep us from sin* (NLV).

Prayer should be offered as an act of worship. How is God to be addressed (verse 9)? "Our _____

in _____..."

Prayer should be offered with great respect. What word describes God's name (verse 9)? "...Your name is

_____."

Prayer should be offered with the future in mind.
What event did God promise to establish in the future
(verse 10)? "May Your _____ _____
come."

Prayer should be offered selflessly. What should be the
desire of your heart (verse 10)? "What You want done,
may it be _____ on _____ as it is
in _____."

Prayer should be offered for personal needs. What did
Jesus say we should ask for (verse 11)? "Give us _____
_____ we _____ _____."

Prayer should be offered for spiritual needs. Write
out the first four words in verse 12. "_____
_____ _____ _____..."

As God has forgiven our sins, what should be our attitude
toward those who hurt us (verse 12)? "...as we
_____ those _____ _____
_____ _____."

Prayer should be about avoiding sin. Write out the first six words in verse 13. "_____ _____

_____ _____ _____ _____..."

Write out what else we should pray for about sin (verse 13). "...but _____ _____ _____ _____."

Beginning Your Journey of Prayer

The best way for you to learn how to pray is by praying. A lot of things are going on in your life at home, at school, and with your friends. So whatever is on your heart and mind is a good place to start talking to God.

But this model that Jesus gave His disciples and us is also a pretty good way to start learning how to pray—in fact, it's perfect!

Do what Jesus said and pray as He prayed:

- Jesus prayed all the time for all things, and so can you.
- Jesus prayed faithfully and sincerely, and so can you.
- Jesus prayed for the good of God's people, and so can you.

So start praying. God is waiting and wanting to hear from you! Follow the advice in Hebrews 4:16:

So let us come boldly to the throne of our gracious God. There we will receive his mercy, and we will find grace to help us when we need it most.

What are some of your concerns or worries? Write them here and then pray about them to God in heaven. He is there, and He is waiting to hear from you.

My concern #1:

_____

_____

My concern #2:

_____

_____

My concern #3:

_____

_____

A PRAYER TO PRAY

Dear God,

I want to have faith in You even though I can't see You or hear You. I do believe You exist, and I am now coming to You with the concerns I have just written out. Thank You for sending Your Son, Jesus, to show me how I need to come to You in prayer with every worry, decision, and choice I make. I look forward to the many blessings that come from talking with You in prayer. Help me to become a young man after Your heart who prays faithfully...just like Jesus did.

Amen.

2

Becoming a Prayer Warrior

What boy grows up not wanting to be someone or something special—to be a superhero? Maybe you want to grow up to be a baseball or soccer star. Some boys want to be firemen, fighter pilots, submarine captains, Navy SEALs or Army Special Forces, or treasure hunters, traveling the world looking for ancient treasure. Other boys dream of being great scientists, doctors, famous chess players, or successful businessmen.

What do all these dreams and goals have in common? Here it is: None of these desires will happen without lots of effort. A baseball star spends years practicing the basics and perfecting his skills as a batter, fielder, or pitcher. The same is true of a soccer star. How many soccer balls do you have to kick toward a goal to become a star? Then there are those who want to be firemen, pilots, or doctors...or to excel at countless other jobs. How many years of training and education are required?

I'm not saying this to discourage your hopes and dreams about your future. What I am saying is that anything you want to do well will require time, training, dedication, and desire. If you want something badly enough, you will do whatever is necessary to accomplish it. To become good at something, you must master everything that the skill requires, and that goes for becoming a prayer warrior too!

Great Men Who Prayed

Why would anyone want to become a prayer warrior? One good reason is that prayer includes all areas of your life. Throughout history, many great generals, men of action, and influential leaders have also been men of prayer. Maybe one of the reasons for their greatness was that prayer was a part of their lives. Just look at the lives of these men!

Abraham was a great desert chieftain. Throughout his life, this extremely powerful man and father of a great nation did not neglect to pray and worship God. In the verse below, *underline* what Abraham did that showed he loved and served God.

> *Then the LORD appeared to Abram [Abraham].... And Abram built an altar there and dedicated it to the LORD.... After that, Abram traveled south and set up camp in the hill country.... There he built another altar and dedicated it to the LORD, and he worshiped the LORD* (Genesis 12:7-8).

Moses was a leader of millions. After leading two million people out of Egypt, Moses was often on his knees, praying for God's direction as he continued leading the nation of Israel. In the verses below, *underline* what Moses was praying for.

*Moses immediately threw himself to the ground and wor-
shiped. And he said, "O Lord, if it is true that I have found
favor with you, then please travel with us"* (Exodus 34:8-9).

David was a great warrior and king who fought many battles. He united the people into a great kingdom, but he was
also a man of prayer. In the prayer below, what was David's
request after he confessed that he had acted foolishly? *Underline* your answer.

*And he said to the LORD, "I have sinned greatly by taking this
census. Please forgive my guilt, LORD, for doing this foolish
thing* (2 Samuel 24:10).

Daniel was a great statesman in ancient Persia. From his
youth Daniel prayed. What was his usual practice each day,
even when he was forbidden to pray? Be sure to *underline* the
answer.

*But when Daniel learned that the law had been signed, he
went home and knelt down as usual in his upstairs room, with
its windows open toward Jerusalem. He prayed three times
a day, just as he had always done, giving thanks to his God*
(Daniel 6:10).

Nehemiah was an important officer in the Persian gov-
ernment. He was also a builder. Nehemiah traveled to Jerusalem to help rebuild the wall around the city. While Nehemiah

was there, his life was constantly threatened. *Underline* the two things he did about these threats.

> *But we prayed to our God and guarded the city day and night to protect ourselves* (Nehemiah 4:9).

Jesus was the Son of God. He was the greatest man who ever lived. He was—and is—God, and yet He always prayed to His Father in heaven. *Underline* what Jesus told His disciples He was going to do to prepare to die on the cross.

> *Sit here while I go and pray* (Mark 14:32).

Developing the Skills of a Prayer Warrior

Another question you might be asking or thinking is, why use the word "warrior" to describe the quiet activity of prayer? Ephesians 6:10-12 has the answer:

> 10 *A final word: Be strong in the Lord and in his mighty power.*
>
> 11 *Put on all of God's armor so that you will be able to stand firm against all strategies of the devil.*
>
> 12 *For we are not fighting against flesh-and-blood enemies, but against evil rulers and authorities of the unseen world, against mighty powers in this dark world, and against evil spirits in the heavenly places.*

In verse 11, *underline* whose strategies we are to stand against.

Our enemies are not people. They are not "flesh-and-blood." In verse 12, *underline* who the real enemies are.

> **JUST A NOTE:** Evil rulers, authorities, mighty powers, and evil spirits are four different levels of demons. We can't see these enemies, but they work for the devil to disrupt the purpose of God. The devil commands these demons, just as a general directs his troops in battle.

Read verse 10 again. What is the first thing we are to do in the fight against the devil and his forces of evil? Write it here and remember it.

"Be _____ in the _____

and in his _____ _____."

According to verse 11, what else are we to do as we stand with our mighty God in the fight against the devil and his forces of evil? Write out the first six words in verse 11.

"_____ _____ _____ _____ _____

_____..."

According to the verse below, what else should we be doing as we do battle with the devil and his forces of evil?

Pray in the Spirit at all times and on every occasion. Stay alert and be persistent in your prayers for all believers everywhere (Ephesians 6:18).

What are you to do? "Pray _____ _____

_____."

When are you to pray?

"...at _____ _____ and on

_____ _____."

What should be your attitude as you pray?

"Stay _____ and be _____..."

Whom should you be praying for?

"...for _____ _____

_____."

Now can you see why we are talking about being a prayer warrior? God is asking you as one of His young men to step up and become a warrior. Be one of His knights in the battle against evil. Prayer is a weapon you can begin to master right now, right where you are, as you grow into the mighty man of valor God wants you to be.

Master the Art of Being a Prayer Warrior

As we said earlier, mastering any area of life—whether in sports or business, or being a policeman, a fireman, a soldier, or one of God's knights—requires time and dedication. The amount of time you spend on something will play a large part in determining how good you become at it.

To become good at something requires daily involvement. So when is a good time each day for you to pray? Jesus was super busy teaching people, healing the sick, and casting out demons. Yet Jesus took time to pray, as we see in Mark 1:35:

Before daybreak the next morning, Jesus got up and went out to an isolated place to pray.

According to this verse, when did Jesus have time to pray?

_____ _____

What do you learn about Jesus' place of prayer? It was an

_____ place.

Jesus gives us a good example of when to pray and where to pray. You can start now to develop the habit of praying before the day gets started. So find a quiet place...and pray. You'll be glad you did!

Your goal is to see prayer as a lifestyle. God wants you to be praying about everyone and everything. And here's good news—you can pray with your voice or in your mind, and you can pray when you're standing, sitting, or kneeling. How you pray is up to you. God only asks you to pray.

Yes, but How?

Here are a few suggestions on how you can develop a habit of prayer in your life.

Start with a commitment: "I'm going to take a few minutes to pray every day for the next five days."

Start with a few minutes first thing each day. Your goal is to pray *before* your day gets too busy.

Start with a few days. Here's a checklist of days to get you started as you spend a few minutes in prayer. Check each day you pray.

____ Day one

____ Day two

____ Day three

____ Day four

____ Day five

Start with a prayer list. All you need is a sheet of paper and a pencil. Then make a list of the people and issues that are important to you and to God. Use this list as a guide during your prayers each day. Some suggestions for your prayer list include...

your parents

your brothers and sisters

your friends

bullies or those who seem to be mad at you

your teachers

your youth leaders and teachers at church

Remember, prayer can be as simple and easy as saying, "Good morning, God. It's me, Ryan. I want to give my day to You and ask You to be with Mom and Dad today. And please help me do well in my schoolwork today. Amen."

End each day with prayer. Thank God for your day and look forward to talking with Him again in the morning!

A PRAYER TO PRAY

Dear God,

I don't know what I want to be when I grow up, but I do want to be something special! I know that whatever it is, it will require lots of hard work—and lots of help from You! Help me to make the effort to become a man who will do great things for You and others. And while I am preparing to be this kind of man, help me to be a boy who is a prayer warrior. I want to be Your boy who does battle with the enemy. Thanks in advance for Your help and for filling me with Your mighty power.

Amen.

When You Have a Bad Attitude... Pray!

Are you a morning person? Some people wake up full of energy, excited to start a new day. Other people...not so much.

I'm guessing that on at least a few occasions, your family members have noticed that you came to the breakfast table with a less-than-happy face. Maybe they said something like, "Boy, you must have gotten up on the wrong side of the bed" or "Here comes Mr. Grumpy," or maybe they nicknamed you "King of the Bad Attitude."

Obviously, you have a real problem if you often show up as Mr. Grumpy Guy. Why is this a problem? Because the Bible says you are to show up as Mr. Happy Guy—a guy with the right attitude.

The Result of a Bad Attitude

A bad attitude always expresses itself in an ugly way, like being grumpy, angry, or impatient. What was the first bad attitude demonstrated by Cain?

"Why are you so angry?" the LORD asked Cain. "Why do you look so dejected?" (Genesis 4:6).

Cain was _____, and he looked

_____ (unhappy).

For some reason, God had rejected Cain's offering, but He had accepted his brother Abel's offering. In Genesis 4:1-5 Cain showed a bad attitude by being angry, and his bad attitude didn't stop with anger. *Circle* what Cain did next in Genesis 4:8.

One day Cain suggested to his brother, "Let's go out into the fields." And while they were in the field, Cain attacked his brother, Abel, and killed him.

Cain's bad attitude moved him to kill his brother, and his bad attitude continued to cause Cain to do other evil things when God asked him about his brother.

Afterward the LORD asked Cain, "Where is your brother? Where is Abel?"

"I don't know," Cain responded. "Am I my brother's guardian?" (Genesis 4:9).

Notice the two sins Cain committed while talking with God in verse 9 and write them here:

_____

_____

_____

You might not think having a bad attitude is a big deal, but as you can see, Cain had a bad attitude after God rejected his offering. He was unhappy and angry, which led him to kill his brother, lie to God, and talk back, or speak disrespectfully, to God. The next time you have a bad attitude, stop and think about Cain.

Your Attitude Begins in Your Heart

You probably know that every computer has a hard drive and an operating system (like Windows or macOS). The hard drive stores data, and the operating system retrieves that data when you need it. Well, your heart is like that. It is the control center of your emotions and actions and attitudes.

The heart must be really important to God because the Bible speaks of the heart almost 1,000 times! Let's look at several verses and see what they say we should do about our hearts. *Circle* what you are to do with your heart, and *underline* why that's important.

> Guard your heart above all else,
> for it determines the course of your life (Proverbs 4:23).

The behavior you exhibit is the overflow of what's going on in your heart. The heart is the control center of your emotions, actions, and attitudes, so watching over your heart is a must. Only you—and no one else—can guard your heart. Not your parents, and not your teachers. It's totally up to you!

"The course of your life" is the direction your life is taking. The writer of Proverbs warns you to check the attitude of your heart because it will determine which way your life will go. A heart that always has a bad attitude will lead you in a bad direction. Again, think about Cain!

Let's look at some other reasons why we must guard our hearts. What two things do you learn about the heart from Jeremiah 17:9?

> *The human heart is the most deceitful of all things,*
> *and desperately wicked.*

"The human heart is the most _____

of all things, and _____ _____."

Read Jeremiah 17:9 again and think back to Cain's life and actions in Genesis 4. Can you see now why you need to guard your heart?

Prayer is a giant help with a bad attitude. According to Psalm 139:23, what should be your prayer?

> *Search me, O God, and know my heart;*
> *test me and know my anxious thoughts* (NIV).

Circle the two things Psalm 139:23 says you can and should ask God to do for you.

God is asking you to take full responsibility for the care of your heart—of your thoughts, actions, and attitudes. Just as your parents take you to the doctor for regular physical examinations, so you should regularly examine your heart. How is this done? Look at a different translation of Proverbs 4:23 and *underline* the answer:

Watch over your heart with all diligence,
For from it flow the springs of life (NASB).

The word "diligence" reminds us of a guard who is on constant duty. This is what happens when you diligently and regularly read your Bible and pray. These two spiritual practices, or disciplines—reading your Bible and praying—place you before God so He can work in your heart. Use the psalmist's words as a model for your own heartfelt prayer: "Search me, O God."

Like the psalmist David, you and I need to pray and ask God to point out anything in our hearts that offends Him. Ask Him to search your heart for any bad attitudes and see if you are committing other sins that displease Him.

Your Attitude Is a Choice

Your parents always give you everything you want, right? Wrong! Parents know that sometimes you want things that aren't helpful. Because they love you, they sometimes have to say no.

Let's find out how God wants you to act when you don't get what you want. How should you respond to something you don't want to do or like doing? And how are you going to act when someone says you must do it anyway? These are the moments when you must make a choice. "Do I respond God's way—with a happy heart—or do I respond with a bad attitude?"

Look again at the story of Cain. God confronted Cain about his bad attitude. What did God say were Cain's choices?

You will be accepted if you do what is right. But if you refuse to do what is right, then watch out! Sin is crouching at the door, eager to control you. But you must subdue it and be its master (Genesis 4:7).

Where is sin? "Sin is _____

_____ _____ _____…"

What is sin ready and waiting to do? "Sin is crouching at the door, _____ to _____

_____."

What must you decide in order to do what is right?

"But you must _____ it and be its

_____."

Unfortunately, Cain chose to continue with his bad attitude, and some terrible things happened! But God wants to show you a better way. As you move into this final section, watch for the letters that spell **J-O-Y**.

Jesus shows you the choice of joy. There is a difference between being happy and being joyful. Happiness is a feeling. If something happens in your life that's good, like getting your way or getting what you want, then you are happy. But if you don't get what you want, then you are unhappy.

Jesus is the perfect example of a person who experienced a lot of bad things. But notice Jesus' attitude even in difficult times:

For the joy set before him he endured the cross, scorning its shame...(Hebrews 12:2 NIV).

What was Jesus' attitude as He faced difficulties, trouble, torture, and death?

"For the _____ set before him he _____

the cross..."

Happiness is what you experience when you are surrounded by fun things or people you like. But *joy* comes as you follow Jesus' example. The joy Jesus possessed and experienced came from His choice to focus on God and trust Him.

Like Jesus, you can experience joy even when you're not surrounded by fun things. Your joy is a choice.

Others show you how to choose to have a good attitude, a joyous attitude. Below are two groups of men who suffered bad things. Use your pencil to write down how these men chose to respond to their troubles.

Example 1: Peter and the other apostles were whipped by the Jewish religious leaders because they preached about Jesus. How did the apostles respond to their beating?

The apostles left the high council rejoicing that God had counted them worthy to suffer disgrace for the name of Jesus (Acts 5:41).

"The apostles left the council _____..."

Why were they rejoicing? Because "God had counted

them _____ to _____...

for the name of Jesus."

Example 2: The apostle Paul and his friend Silas were whipped and thrown into jail for preaching about Jesus. Write out their response to being chained up, and the response of their fellow prisoners.

Around midnight Paul and Silas were praying and singing hymns to God, and the other prisoners were listening (Acts 16:25).

"...Paul and Silas were _____ and

_____ _____ to

_____..."

What was the response of their fellow prisoners?

"...the other prisoners were _____."

Take a minute and think back to something your parents wanted you to do, like cleaning your room, or taking out the trash, or something else you didn't want to do. How did you respond to that unpleasant task?

_____

_____

_____

The next time you are asked to do something, what will you say and do? Or, put another way, what choice will you make?

_____

_____

_____

Yield to God. To yield means to give in or to submit to someone else's power. Think again about Cain's life.

You will be accepted if you do what is right. But if you refuse to do what is right, then watch out! Sin is crouching at the door, eager to control you (Genesis 4:7).

Whom did Cain yield his life to? To _____

To yield to God means to obey Him, to do things His way. How can these verses help you know what God wants you to do?

You can pray and seek God's help. God wants to help you deal with your bad attitudes, but you must ask for His help. As Psalm 105:4 instructs,

*Search for the L*ORD *and for his strength;
continually seek him.*

Today I will...

_____

_____

You can read your Bible. List some things these verses from Psalm 119 say you can do to keep from having a bad attitude.

⁹ *How can a young person stay pure?*
By obeying your word.

¹⁰ *I have tried hard to find you—*
don't let me wander from your commands.

¹¹ *I have hidden your word in my heart,*
that I might not sin against you.

Verse 9—By...

_____

_____

Verse 10—Don't...

_____

_____

Verse 11—Hide...

_____

_____

Yes, but How?

In this chapter we have looked at what happens when you have a bad attitude and don't choose to turn that bad attitude into an attitude of **JOY**. Look back at the three letters that spell **JOY**. Write out the point of each letter.

Jesus shows you...

_____

Others show you...

_____

_____

Yield _____ _____.

A PRAYER TO PRAY

O God,

It's tough to admit, but I agree with Your Word that my heart is sinful. I want to do what is right and have a good attitude You want me to have, but I often fail. I hurt others with my ugly words, actions, and bad attitudes. I know these actions don't please You, and I ask for Your forgiveness as I move on in my desire to choose to have a good attitude. As I've learned in this lesson, please search my heart and see what's keeping me from obeying You and doing what pleases You.

Amen.

4

When It Comes to Family... Pray!

Did you know God created you to be a social being? He wants you to enjoy being around people. For instance, think of the people where you live. You have parents and probably some brothers and sisters. (You may also have a dog or cat the family treats like a person!) Every person who lives under your roof is a person you have a relationship with. That means they are people you can—and should—pray for.

There are at least three ways you can pray for Mom and Dad and others who are important to you. These three kinds of prayer will help you continue with your adventure of learning about prayer.

Personal Prayer

This is the kind of prayer where you have a time and place to pray, and when that time comes, you stop what you are doing and sit down and pray. For this personal prayer time, it's good to pray before you leave your room in the morning.

During this time of prayer, even if it's just a few minutes, you stop thinking about what you're going to do that day and focus your thoughts on God and on praying for others—for your parents and brothers and sisters.

If you don't have a journal, ask your parents to help you find or buy one that can become your personal prayer journal. And if you can't get one, staple some notebook paper together. Then put some cool designs on the pages. Maybe you can draw a figure of a soldier—a prayer warrior—on the front page and pray away!

In your journal, list the names of the people you want to pray for. For example, have a special page for Mom and one for Dad. You can do the same for each brother and sister. And don't forget a page to list what you need to pray about for yourself!

The apostle Paul had some very special people in his life who lived in a town called Ephesus. He wrote to them,

> *Ever since I first heard of your strong faith in the Lord Jesus and your love for God's people everywhere, I have not stopped thanking God for you. I pray for you constantly...*(Ephesians 1:15-16).

How often did Paul pray for them?

"I _____ for you _____..."

Right now jot down the names of the family members you want to pray for every day.

_____

_____

_____

_____

_____

Stop-and-Pray-Now Prayers

This is a different kind of prayer because it is not planned. It's not on your schedule. These prayers are usually about something urgent. Here's an example from my life this week. My wife and I were in Hawaii when we received alerts on our cell phones that a ballistic missile had been fired at Hawaii and that we should take cover immediately.

Talk about urgent! Before we even finished reading the alert and warning of danger, we were praying. We prayed for safety for all the people on the Hawaiian Islands. We prayed that people would not be injured or killed. We prayed that God would use this incident to cause people to think about their relationship with the Lord.

And guess what? Fifteen minutes later we received alerts letting us know the threat was not real. Someone had pushed a button by mistake!

There are many kinds of stop-and-pray-now events. When

you hear someone you know is in the hospital, you stop and pray. When you see a car wreck, you pray right then. If you hear your brother or sister or parents arguing, you pray...and pray...and pray. No matter what happens, you can rush to God for His help, His comfort, His wisdom, His guidance, and His peace. There are lots of times during each day when you can stop and pray.

- You can stop and pray silently before you take a test at school.
- You can stop and pray before you eat.
- You can stop and pray silently when your class at church begins.
- You can stop and pray when you go to the doctor...or the dentist!
- You can stop and pray to your heavenly Father no matter where you are or what's happening.

Can you think of a time when something surprising happened and you prayed?

_____

_____

_____

Many people in the Bible offered up "stop-and-pray-now" prayers.

Nehemiah prayed when he was confronted by the King.

So the king asked me, "Why are you looking so sad? You don't look sick to me. You must be deeply troubled." Then I was terrified…With a prayer to the God of heaven, I replied, "If it please the king, and if you are pleased with me, your servant, send me to Judah to rebuild the city where my ancestors are buried" (Nehemiah 2:2-5).

Underline what Nehemiah did when he was terrified by the challenge of the king.

Nehemiah worked for the king of Persia, and he was sad. Why? Because the wall around Jerusalem had been destroyed and its people were in trouble. Everyone knew the king did not like people to be sad around him. Nehemiah feared that his sadness or his request would anger the king and lead to Nehemiah's death, so he uttered a quick prayer to God for help!

What happened? God answered Nehemiah's prayer, and Nehemiah went to Jerusalem, where he and the people rebuilt the wall around Jerusalem in only 52 days!

King Hezekiah, the king of Judah, received a letter saying Jerusalem, the capital city, was surrounded by a foreign army. This enemy threatened to destroy everything and everyone unless Hezekiah surrendered. *Underline* what Hezekiah did in verse 14 and *circle* what he did in verse 15.

¹⁴ *After Hezekiah received the letter from the messengers and read it, he went up to the LORD's Temple and spread it out before the LORD.*

¹⁵ *And Hezekiah prayed this prayer before the LORD: "O LORD, God of Israel, you are enthroned between the mighty cherubim! You alone are God of all the kingdoms of the earth. You alone created the heavens and the earth"* (2 Kings 19:14-15).

Hezekiah prayed for God's help, and God answered his prayer a few days later when the angel of the Lord killed 185,000 enemies in their camp. The enemies who survived left and never returned!

Praying Always

This third type of prayer is sort of like keeping a running conversation going with God. You are thinking about Him. You are talking to Him in your heart. You may even be humming or singing a song about Him in your mind.

In the verses below, *underline* how often God's Word says you should be thinking about God and praying.

The name of the Lord is to be praised from the time the sun rises to when it sets (Psalm 113:3 NLV).

I praise You seven times a day, because Your Law is right (Psalm 119:164 NLV).

Never stop praying (1 Thessalonians 5:17 NLV).

You must keep praying. Keep watching! Be thankful always (Colossians 4:2 NLV).

Now *circle* the verse you want to remember this week.

Getting Along with Your Parents

Now that we have thought about the types of prayers we can offer up to God, here are some Bible verses that will help you as you pray for a better relationship with your parents. *Underline* what God wants you to do in your relationship with your parents.

Children, obey your parents in everything. The Lord is pleased when you do (Colossians 3:20 NLV).

What happens when you obey your parents?

"The Lord _____ _____ when you do."

Wow! This is important! By doing the one thing this verse says to do—obeying your parents—you please your parents and the Lord! Now read Ephesians 6:1-3:

¹ *Children, as Christians, obey your parents. This is the right thing to do.*

² *Respect your father and mother. This is the first Law given that had a promise.*

³ *The promise is this: If you respect your father and mother,*

you will live a long time and your life will be full of many good things (NLV).

What does verse 1 say about obeying your parents?

"This is the _____ _____ to do."

In addition to obeying your parents, what does verse 2 say you are also to do?

"_____ your father and mother."

According to verse 3, how is your life blessed when you obey and respect your parents?

"...you will live ____ _____ _____

and your life will be _____ of _____

_____ _____."

This is another wow! When you obey God's command to respect and honor your parents, God promises you a special blessing!

Here's a checklist that will help you do what God asks you to do—to obey and respect your parents. It will also help you get along with your parents better. Check the ones you will work on.

I WILL

I will honor my parents by showing them respect.

Yes _____   No _____

I will turn to my parents for wisdom and guidance.

Yes _____   No _____

I will learn to genuinely listen to what my parents are trying to tell me.

Yes _____   No _____

I will initiate the process of resolving conflicts with my parents.

Yes _____   No _____

I will express my appreciation to my parents for what they've done for me.

Yes _____   No _____[1]

Getting Along with Your Brothers and Sisters

If you're like most kids, you have to work at having a great relationship with your brothers and sisters. Each one of these family members needs your prayers and your love. An old saying reminds us, "You cannot hate those you are praying for." Prayer turns bad feelings toward a sibling into an opportunity to show and express love. If you have brothers and sisters, remember that God has given them to you as gifts. They are a special part of His plan for you. And He expects you to love and enjoy them—and especially to pray for them.

Circle the word "must" and *underline* each time God says, "love each other." These are commands God wants you to obey.

I give you a new Law. You are to love each other. You must love each other as I have loved you. If you love each other, all men will know you are My followers (John 13:34-35 NLV).

A PRAYER TO PRAY

Father God,

Thank You that I can pray and talk to You, the God of the whole world! All through the Bible You tell Your people to pray, and I want to be more faithful to do just that—to pray. I also see how important it is to You that I love and obey my parents, and that I respect and honor them. Help me as I work on treating my parents the way You want me to treat them. I also want to be a good brother who is kind and prays for my brothers and sisters. I love You, Lord. Help me love my family.

Amen.

5

When It Comes to Friends... Pray!

You may be one of those guys who never met a stranger. You can talk to anyone and make friends easily. Or you may have a longtime childhood friend, and the two of you are always together. But for a lot of guys, it's not easy to find a good friend. So whether you have many friends or a few, we need to begin this discussion on friendships by (you guessed it!) talking about prayer.

Because friendships are a two-way street, the first thing you need to do is pray for your own spiritual growth. Why? If you want a good and godly friend, you must first *be* a good and godly friend. Being a friend starts with praying and asking God to make you the kind of guy who will be a good friend—a friend who can encourage and help another guy.

The second thing you need to do is pray that the friends you make will love God like you do. For-real friends encourage each other in their walk with the Lord.

What Does It Take to Be a Good Friend?

Prayer is the starting point in being a friend and finding and having friends, right? So, what should you be asking God?

Search me, O God, and know my heart...(Psalm 139:23).

You are asking God to search your _____.

As you and God look at your heart, here's what you hope and want to find...

A friend is loyal at all times.

A friend is always loyal,
and a brother is born to help in time of need
(Proverbs 17:17).

Have you ever had a friend show up and come to your aid when you needed help? What did he do to help you?

_____

_____

_____

_____

Now turn this around. Have you ever helped a friend? What did you do for your friend?

_____

_____

_____

_____

As Proverbs 17:17 says, "A friend is always loyal." What will you do the next time one of your friends needs help?

_____

_____

_____

_____

A friend will not sacrifice a friendship to be in a "cool" or popular group. A cool group is also called a clique. A clique is a group of kids who spend all their time together and don't include others. A real problem comes when the people inside the group become mean and believe they are better than the outsiders.

Suppose one of these groups asked you to be part of their group but didn't ask your best friend? What would you do?

_____

_____

_____

Here's something to think about: What if you were part of a cool group of kids. Would Jesus fit into your group?

Was Jesus concerned about being part of a cool group? No, Jesus was "a friend of tax collectors and other sinners" (Luke 7:34).

Like Jesus, you probably know how it feels to be avoided, ignored, criticized, excluded, and overlooked by others. Don't be guilty of treating others this way because...

A friend will always be nice. You've probably heard of the Golden Rule. It says, "Do to others as you would like them to do to you" (Luke 6:31). Did you know Jesus was the person who said this?

Also, did you know the Bible never tells you to just be nice? Here's what it does say:

Instead, be kind to each other, tenderhearted, forgiving one another...(Ephesians 4:32).

How are you to treat everybody, including your friends?

_____

_____

_____

_____

Grade your behavior on these qualities (A, B, or C):

___ kind

___ tenderhearted (or caring)

___ forgiving others

A friend will not talk about his friend to others. A true friend keeps important personal information secret. When you talk about a friend behind his back, this is called gossip or slander. The Bible has a lot to say about slander, what it says about a slander, and how it harms friendships.

...slandering others makes you a fool (Proverbs 10:18).

What does the Bible call someone who can't keep a secret?

"...slandering others makes you a _____."

A gossip goes around telling secrets,
but those who are trustworthy can keep a confidence [a
secret] (Proverbs 11:13).

What does a gossip do? "A gossip goes around telling

_____..."

And what about "those who are trustworthy"?

They "can _____ ___ _____."

A friend will talk about Jesus. The best thing you can do for anyone is to tell them about your friend Jesus. Talking about Him makes you the best friend you can be! Jot down a few notes about how Jesus has been a good friend to you.

Then pray for chances to share with your friends what you have written.

_____

_____

_____

_____

_____

Look again through this chapter and review the heart qualities you need to be a good friend. Then write down the one you need to work on the most. Start praying each day, asking God to help you strengthen that quality.

"God, please help me with this quality that will make me a better friend":

_____

How to Pray for Good Friends

Friends are important! You will have some friends for years, even into your adult years. And others will come and go. God knows this. In fact, He gives you guidelines and principles for choosing your friends and keeping your friends. Your goal is not to have friends, but to have *the right kind* of friends. God's Word is very clear about what you should be praying for as you seek and make friends.

Pray to Be Patient

Finding a friend takes time. Don't be in a hurry. Why? Because you already have friends. For instance...

Jesus is your friend. If you are a Christian, you have a very special friend in Jesus. Jesus said this to His disciples and to you as well: "You are my friends..." (John 15:14). What do these next two verses tell you about your friend Jesus?

> *And be sure of this: I am with you always, even to the end of the age* (Matthew 28:20).

Jesus is "with you _____."

> *I will never fail you.*
> *I will never abandon you* (Hebrews 13:5).

Jesus "will never _____ you."

Jesus "will never _____ you."

If Jesus were your only friend, He would be all you need. But Jesus wants you to have other friends too.

You have friends in your parents. No one loves you more or cares about you more than your parents. Ask God to help you love your parents and develop a forever friendship with them.

And here's a good verse to remember when your parents discipline you:

Wounds from a sincere friend are better than many kisses from an enemy (Proverbs 27:6).

You have friends in your brothers and sisters. It may be a little hard today to see your brothers and sisters as friends, but as you love them and pray for them, spend time with them, and do things together, they will be your friends for life.

Pray for Wisdom

Choosing a friend is one of the most important decisions you can make. How can you know you're making the right choice? Ask God to help you, and discover how the Bible says to make wise choices about your friends.

The Bible is specific about the kind of person to look for as a friend—and the kind to avoid. Here's a list of people God tells you to avoid as friends.

Walk with the wise and become wise;
associate with fools and get in trouble (Proverbs 13:20).

A wise friend causes me to become _____,

but a foolish "friend" causes me to _____ _____

_____.

Don't befriend angry people
or associate with hot-tempered people…(Proverbs 22:24).

I'm not to be friends with _____ people,

and not to associate with _____ -_____

people.

Do not be misled: "Bad company corrupts good character" (1 Corinthians 15:33 NIV).

What effect do the wrong kind of friends have on you?

_____

_____

Pray for Spiritually Mature Friends

You are already praying to grow spiritually, and you should be looking for friends who are also growing in the Lord. If you desire to grow spiritually and know more about God and how He wants you to act, you will want to have friends who share your desire to grow, right?

*The godly give good advice to their friends;
the wicked lead them astray* (Proverbs 12:26).

In your own words, why should you want godly friends?

_____

_____

_____

_____

Pray to Be Like Daniel

Daniel was not much older than you are now when he was taken away from his homeland and family to a faraway land. But instead of becoming like everyone around him, Daniel chose to stand up for his beliefs. For example, Daniel determined not to defile himself by eating the food and drinking the wine given to those who were being trained to serve the king. Daniel asked for and received permission not to eat those unacceptable foods (Daniel 1:5-8).

And guess what? Are you surprised that Daniel chose friends who were strong in their faith as well? Their names were Shadrach, Meshach, and Abednego. When these three young men were ordered to kneel and worship a false god, what did they say and do?

17 *If we are thrown into the blazing furnace, the God whom we serve is able to save us. He will rescue us from your power, Your Majesty.*

18 *But even if he doesn't, we want to make it clear to you, Your Majesty, that we will never serve your gods or worship the gold statue you have set up* (Daniel 3:17-18).

"...we will never _____ _____

_____..." (verse 18).

These, my young brother in Christ, are the kind of friends you must look for and pray to find. Be bold like Daniel was.

Know what the Bible says and do it. Be strong in your faith and surround yourself with friends who are also strong in the Lord.

If you are wondering where you will find friends who will stand strong when it comes to doing what is right, here's a hint: You will usually find these friends at church or in a youth Bible study.

A PRAYER TO PRAY

Dear Jesus,

Thank You for being my forever friend and for Your promise to never leave me. I also want to thank You for my parents. Help me to love them more and more and to go to them when I have problems. Also, please help me love my brothers and sisters and be their close friend. Please give me Your wisdom as I look for friends who love You as I do. When I find them, may I be a loyal and faithful friend to them. I want to be a friend who encourages my friends.

Amen.

6

When You Must Make a Decision... Pray!

Most young guys look forward to getting older. You probably do too. Why? Because there are so many cool things you will be able to do—like throw a football farther, kick a soccer ball more accurately, and do many other activities that require physical maturity. And just think, you'll be able to drive a car! You won't need Mom to take you to your friends' houses or school activities. I'll bet you can hardly wait!

Here's another important activity that comes with age—making decisions on your own. Right now, you're making small decisions, but most of the major decisions are being made by your parents. So as you wait patiently for the future to hurry up and get here, you can begin developing your decision-making skills. Your future success starts with the decisions you make right now, right where you are, at your present age.

You Don't Need to Pray About Some Decisions

The primary guidebook for life and decision-making will always be the Bible. It has clear guidance for most decisions you face every day.

Any decision that disobeys your parents is out.

Children, obey your parents because you belong to the Lord, for this is the right thing to do (Ephesians 6:1).

Your parents have said, "Don't leave the house or yard without letting us know." What should be your response when your friends ask you to grab your bike and join them for a ride? How should you answer?

_____

Any decision that disrespects your parents is out.

"Honor your father and mother." This is the first commandment with a promise...(Ephesians 6:2).

You've seen your friends talk back, argue, and say ugly things to their parents. What should you do when your mom or dad asks you to do something you don't want to do?

_____

_____

Any decision that disobeys God's Word is out. For example, the Bible makes clear that you are not to lie, steal, and say bad words.

The LORD detests lying lips,
but he delights in those who tell the truth (Proverbs 12:22).

You must not steal (Romans 13:9).

Don't use foul or abusive language (Ephesians 4:29).

Some of your friends lie to their parents. What should you do differently?

_____

_____

Your friends want you to help them steal some candy at the corner market. What should you do?

_____

_____

Any decision that disobeys authority is out. God has put people in your life to keep you safe and help you grow. These include teachers and law enforcement officers.

For the Lord's sake, submit to all human authority...(1 Peter 2:13).

Your teacher asked the class not to mark on the desks. What should you do?

_____

_____

Any decision that would harm your body is out. What do you think the Bible has to say about using cigarettes, alcohol, or drugs?

> *Don't you realize that your body is the temple of the Holy Spirit, who lives in you and was given to you by God? You do not belong to yourself, for God bought you with a high price. So you must honor God with your body* (1 Corinthians 6:19-20).

Someone in your class has a cigarette or a small amount of a prescription drug, and they ask you to participate with them. What should you say and do?

_____

Any decision that goes against the standards God sets in the Bible is a no-brainer. You don't even need to pray about it. The answer to anything like this must be no. Don't do it!

No Other Decision Made Without Prayer

We've seen that a lot of decisions are black-and-white. The Bible clearly shows that they are either right or wrong.

But not all the decisions you will have to make are like that. For instance, what about decisions about your attitude? Or how you spend your free time or your money? When you must make decisions like these, you should always start with prayer.

The Bible has many examples of people who made decisions without praying first. Look at what happened to these people who didn't pray or consult God before making their decisions.

Eve ate the forbidden fruit. The serpent told Eve, "You won't die!…God knows that your eyes will be opened as soon as you eat it, and you will be like God, knowing both good and evil" (Genesis 3:4-5). So Eve decided to eat the fruit that was offered by the serpent, which resulted in sin entering the world.

King Saul did not wait for the prophet Samuel. Samuel had instructed Saul to wait for Samuel to come and offer a sacrifice. But Saul was afraid his men would leave him if he waited for Samuel, so he offered the sacrifice himself. When Samuel arrived, he said to the king, "You have not kept the command the LORD your God gave you.… Now your kingdom must end, for the LORD has sought out a man after his own heart" (1 Samuel 13:13-14). Saul's poor decision cost him the kingdom.

King Rehoboam listened to the wrong people (see 1 Kings 12:5-8). What happened? The nation's leaders came to Rehoboam and asked him to lower their taxes. Rather than going to God in prayer or seeking wisdom from godly, mature men, he took the advice of some of his childhood buddies. His poor decision divided the kingdom and resulted in civil war.

Eve, King Saul, and King Rehoboam made wrong decisions because they didn't pray and ask God for guidance.

Can you remember a decision you made without any help or guidance from God or your parents? Jot down what the decision was about.

_____

_____

_____

What were the results? What would you do differently now, and why?

_____

_____

_____

After reading about the bad decisions Eve, King Saul, and King Rehoboam made and seeing the results, what should be your first thought before making a decision?

No _____ made without

_____.

Here are several examples of men and women who show us the *positive* results of praying *before* making decisions.

Nehemiah prayed for guidance.

When I heard this [that the walls in Jerusalem were down], I sat down and wept. In fact, for days I mourned, fasted, and prayed to the God of heaven (Nehemiah 1:4).

Nehemiah was working for the king of Persia when he heard about the problems the people were having in Jerusalem. What did he do to get help?

He "_____ to the God of heaven."

God answered Nehemiah's prayers, and the king allowed him to go to Jerusalem and rebuild the wall around the city, giving God's people protection from their enemies.

Jesus prayed for direction.

35 *Before daybreak the next morning, Jesus got up and went out to an isolated place to pray.*

36 *Later Simon and the others went out to find him.*

37 *When they found him, they said, "Everyone is looking for you."*

38 *But Jesus replied, "We must go on to other towns as well, and I will preach to them, too. That is why I came"* (Mark 1:35-38).

In verse 35, how did the Lord Jesus seek His Father's direction for His ministry?

"...Jesus got up and went out to an isolated place to

_____."

After seeing how God blessed these people who prayed before making decisions, what will you do the next time you need to make a decision? (It helps to have a page in your prayer notebook or journal titled "Decisions to Make.")

I will...

_____

_____

Prayer Helps You Make Wise Decisions

Even though you are probably younger than you want to be, there are many decisions you make every day. The issue is not whether you are allowed to make decisions, because you are *already* making many decisions, with or without your parents' input and approval. But wouldn't it be great to have God's help in making the right and wisest decisions? Prayer gives you that help!

We have seen that some decisions need no prayer because God's Word already tells us what we are to do. And we've seen that other everyday decisions require God's input. Daily living demands that we are constantly praying because...

Prayer is how you seek God's wisdom. We don't receive wisdom automatically. You are not born with wisdom. If you want wisdom, you must ask for it!

If you need wisdom, ask our generous God, and he will give it to you. He will not rebuke you for asking (James 1:5).

Prayer is how you continue in wisdom. Prayer shows your dependence on God and respect for Him. Every prayer you pray proves your respect for God. It also continues God's flow of wisdom to guide your decisions.

> *Fear of the LORD is the foundation of wisdom.*
> *Knowledge of the Holy One results in good judgment*
> (Proverbs 9:10).

Prayer keeps you from making foolish decisions. Respecting and honoring God enough to pray for wisdom will keep you from making foolish decisions.

> *Fear of the LORD is the foundation of true knowledge,*
> *but fools despise wisdom and discipline* (Proverbs 1:7).

Prayer helps you see things from God's point of view. God wants you to be wise and to make wise choices. Unfortunately, some people in the Bible didn't make wise decisions, and they are called fools. Here's a list of the actions of fools according to the book of Proverbs:

> The fool envies others.
>
> The fool doesn't seek advice.
>
> The fool cannot get along with others.
>
> The fool wastes his money.
>
> The fool is always angry.
>
> The fool lies.

If you want to set yourself apart from the "fools" that surround you at school and in your neighborhood, pray. Prayer will set you on the path of wisdom.

Prayer Will Help in Your Understanding

It cannot be explained, but when you pray—when you talk to God and wait for His direction—you do receive direction. As you pray and read your Bible, you begin to understand how to make decisions that please God. Read God's promise to give you understanding in Proverbs 3:5-6:

> ⁵ Trust in the LORD with all your heart;
>   do not depend on your own understanding.
> ⁶ Seek his will in all you do,
>   and he will show you which path to take.

What are the three pieces of advice God gives you regarding your decisions?

Verse 5: "Trust in the _____ with _____

_____ _____..."

Verse 5: "...do not depend on your _____

_____."

Verse 6: "Seek his will _____ _____ _____

_____..."

Verse 6: What is God's part? "...and he will

_____ you which _____ to take."

King Solomon prayed, "Give me an understanding heart so that I can govern your people well and know the difference between right and wrong" (1 Kings 3:9).

What did Solomon ask for from God?

King Solomon prayed for "an _____

_____."

Why did he ask for this?

So he could _____ the people

and know the difference between _____ and

_____.

No wonder King Solomon became the wisest man of his time!

As a boy after God's own heart, trust God. Don't look to your own understanding. Seek *God's* understanding, and He will help you grow into a wise man who makes wise decisions.

A PRAYER TO PRAY

Dear Lord,

You are my Shepherd. Please guide me as one of Your sheep toward good and right decisions. I have a long way to go, Lord, but I want to follow You. I am excited to start paying more attention to the choices I make. I want to make decisions that please You. I know and believe that You will guide me in making wise decisions.

Amen.

7

When You Need Courage... Pray!

We all have fears, even though we wouldn't dare admit them to our friends. If you did, you might be labeled a fraidy-cat, and how embarrassing would that be!

When I was in my early teens, I read the book *The Red Badge of Courage* by Stephen Crane. It is about an 18-year-old boy who joined the army during the Civil War. During his first battle, he became afraid and fled. The book followed his journey from being a coward to becoming a young man with the courage to return to the battle. He was still fearful, but his newfound courage prompted him to become the standard-bearer who proudly carried his unit's flag in front of the army without a weapon in hand.

How to Handle Fear

The Red Badge of Courage is inspiring, but the Bible provides even more powerful examples of courage. Read on to see how prayer gave David courage. *Underline* what David did when he was afraid.

I prayed to the LORD, and he answered me.
He freed me from all my fears (Psalm 34:4).

After David prayed, what did the Lord do?

"...and he _____ me. He freed

me _____ _____ _____ _____."

When you are fearful like David was, what two things can you count on from God?

God will _____ your prayers, and

God will _____ you from all your _____.

Look at Psalm 34:4 again. According to what we have just learned, what should be your first response when you are afraid? You should _____.

Now read this verse from David and fill in the blanks.

God is our refuge and strength,
always ready to help in times of trouble (Psalm 46:1).

"God is our _____ and

_____..."

Because God is your refuge and strength, what is God ready to do in times of trouble?

He is "always ready _____ _____."

David also tells us what it takes to be a boy after God's own heart. God says, "I have found David…a man after my own heart. He will do everything I want him to do" (Acts 13:22).

What made David a man after God's own heart?

"He _____ do _____

I want him to do."

Let's review: What do you now know about God that helps you as you pray?

God _____ our prayers (Psalm 34:4).

God is our _____ and

_____ (Psalm 46:1).

God is ready to _____ us in times of trouble

(Psalm 46:1).

Fear Is Not a Bad Thing

Fear is the right response for many things. You should fear strangers, traffic, fire, and so on. You should also fear the influence of hanging out with the wrong crowd at school.

Fear is also a good thing when it comes to respecting and honoring God. Just as you are to honor and respect your parents, you are also to honor God. *Circle* or *underline* the words that describe what happens when you love, honor, and respect God—when you fear Him.

> *For the angel of the LORD is a guard;*
> *he surrounds and defends all who fear him* (Psalm 34:7).

> *Fear of the LORD is the foundation of true knowledge…* (Proverbs 1:7).

> *Fear of the LORD leads to life,*
> *bringing security and protection from harm* (Proverbs 19:23).

What can you do right now—and anytime—to show that you fear God, that you honor and respect Him? (Hint: What is this book about?)

I can _____.

Another thing you can do is obey your parents. You show that you love and respect God by obeying His Word when it says,

> *Children, obey your parents because you belong to the Lord, for this is the right thing to do. "Honor your father and mother." This is the first commandment with a promise: If you honor your father and mother, "things will go well for you, and you will have a long life on the earth"* (Ephesians 6:1-3).

In the verses above, *underline* two or three reasons you should obey your parents.

Courage in the Face of Fear

We've seen that Nehemiah prayed to God for protection as he and the Jewish people were surrounded by their enemies while working to rebuild the wall around Jerusalem. Nehemiah was fearful, but with God's help, he was also courageous. What helped him be courageous? Every time there was a problem, Nehemiah prayed. I hope Nehemiah's faith in God and his habit of prayer will remind you what to do the next time you are fearful.

Here's something I wrote about Nehemiah and about courage in a book for men. I like Nehemiah because he wasn't a priest or military man—just a guy like you and me. But what made him special was that prayer was always his first response to any problem. Since you are becoming a man—a knight in God's army and a prayer warrior in the making—this will help you understand what it means to have courage.

"Courage...does not dismiss fear. It evaluates the cause for the fear and determines how to proceed. Courage may choose to stand and fight with fear as its companion. Or...it may well choose to retreat in order to fight another day."[2]

A Man Who Needed Courage

Meet Joshua. Joshua was a warrior who took over the leadership of God's people from Moses just before they were to enter the Promised Land. Joshua had never had such an important leadership role—he was responsible for more than two million people. He was supposed to lead them into a new land, but there was just one problem. The people in the Promised Land were big, strong, and numerous, and they didn't want to give up their land. This would make any new leader a little fearful.

As you read about Joshua, you will quickly discover he had a bad case of fear. Let's see how God changed Joshua's fear into courage in Joshua 1:7-9:

> **Verse 7**: *Be strong and very courageous. Be careful to obey all the instructions Moses gave you. Do not deviate from them, turning either to the right or to the left. Then you will be successful in everything you do.*

The first thing Joshua was told to do was to "be strong

and _____ _____."

Next God told Joshua, "Be careful to _____ all the instructions Moses gave you."

Then God warned Joshua, "Do not _____ from them..."

If Joshua would do these things, God promised him,

"Then you will be _____ in

_____ you do."

Verse 8: *Study this Book of Instruction continually. Meditate on it day and night so you will be sure to obey everything written in it. Only then will you prosper and succeed in all you do.*

You may not want to hear this again, but to be good at anything, you must study, grow, and learn. In verse 8, what does God say Joshua needed to do in order to have success?

"_____this Book of Instruction [the Bible]

_____."

You will have to study in school to be successful in whatever you want to do when you grow up. It is also true that if you want to be successful as God's warrior, or God's knight, who goes into the world to fight the forces of evil, you are going to have to read your Bible. God wants you not only to read and study your Bible but also to obey what you are reading.

Verse 9: *This is my command—be strong and courageous! Do not be afraid or discouraged. For the LORD your God is with you wherever you go.*

This is the third time God told Joshua to be strong and courageous (see Joshua 1:6-7,9). God then adds these words of comfort:

"Do not be _____ or

_____."

How can Joshua do this? Look again at verse 9, where God says,

"For the LORD your God is _____ you

_____ you go."

Courage in God's Presence

Jesus said, "And be sure of this: I am with you always, even to the end of the age" (Matthew 28:20). Friend, you don't have to be fearful! Ever! Why? Because Jesus promised,

"...I am with you _____..."

You can be courageous because you know that Jesus is always nearby—right there with you—no matter what happens and no matter where you go. This was also a secret to Joshua's courage—God was right there with him. And courage can be yours, too, as you make your way through every trial and difficulty, trusting and believing and knowing that God is right there with you.

What Does Courage Look Like?

My friend, courage doesn't just happen. Courage grows as you...

- pray,
- read your Bible,
- understand God's presence in your life, and

- count on His ability to guide you and keep you safe.

Trust God in the little things, and He will give you courage in the big things. So, what does courage look like?

Courage takes a stand. Other boys may try to bully you into doing things the Bible and your parents tell you are wrong. These include lying, stealing, and rebelling against authority. But God will give you courage to stand against those who want you to join them in doing bad things.

Courage makes the right choices. Fear of rejection and fear of not being popular can cause you to make wrong choices. But courage helps you make right choices, even if those choices are unpopular. Listen to God and your parents. They are the ones you need to please.

Courage does not compromise. God has given you His Word, the Bible. Every problem you will ever face has its answer in the Bible. Your classmates and neighborhood friends may want you to ignore what the Bible says and do things that are popular, immoral, and even illegal. But courage will not be swayed from the truth of God's Word.

Yes, but How?

How did men of God like David, Nehemiah, and Joshua find courage? It's hard to have courage if you don't know what you are supposed to do. These three men gained courage as they prayed and read and obeyed God's Word. And the same is true for you. To "be successful in everything you do" (Joshua 1:7), pray, read your Bible, and do what it says.

So whether you are sitting in the dentist's chair today or standing in front of your class giving a report—or someday flying a fighter jet at 600 miles an hour or navigating a submarine with 600 feet of water above you—know this: The mighty God of the universe is right there with you! That's pretty special, isn't it?

What's happening in your day and your life? Whatever you are facing, pray. Ask God for courage as you face today, tomorrow, and next week. Know that He is beside you as you deal with every challenge.

In the blanks below, list what's coming up in your next few days or weeks. Then pray and thank God that He is beside you to help you every step of the way.

"God, here are some tough areas, issues, and people in my life. Give me courage to face these people and problems and handle them Your way."

_____

_____

_____

_____

_____

_____

A PRAYER TO PRAY

Dear God,

I know I shouldn't be afraid, but I admit there are times when I am. Thank You that You are by my side at all times to protect me. Give me the courage to obey what I read in my Bible. Help me stand up for what I believe, even if other kids laugh and make fun of me. I want to rely on Your strength and be strong in You and Your power. I want to be a boy who is courageous, a boy who does what is right, whatever the cost. This is my prayer, O Lord.

Amen.

8

When It Comes to Trouble or Needs... Pray!

Don't go looking for trouble!
        Why?

Because whether you like it or not, trouble will find you. This is a fact of life, even for a young guy like you. We are not talking about the trouble that comes when you are caught in a lie to your parents, or the trouble you get into for talking in class when you know you're not supposed to. No, we are going to talk about the trouble or trials that happen to everyone, including strong Christians. What are you supposed to do when these challenges arrive? James has advice for you:

> *Dear brothers and sisters, when troubles of any kind come your way, consider it an opportunity for great joy* (James 1:2).

As James wrote about trials and troubles in life, he did not say *if* troubles come your way. "If" means that troubles might come your way, or they might not. But James said, "...*when* troubles of any kind come your way," which means trials are a certainty—even a *daily* possibility!

Since trouble can occur daily, what are you to do? Or what can you do?

This is where prayer comes to your rescue. Don't make the mistake of thinking you can meet trouble head-on, that you can take it in stride, that you can handle your problems on your own. Instead, look up and reach out to your all-powerful heavenly Father for help!

In Times of Trouble...Pray!

Here's something that's important to remember about prayer: Don't wait until you've done something wrong and then pray to God to get you out of your mess. But whenever you face a big problem, you can use sincere and urgent prayer to ask for God's help...like these people did:

Nehemiah faced trouble. As we have already noted Nehemiah was a man of prayer. He prayed for God to give him guidance, and God guided him to Jerusalem to rebuild the city wall. While Nehemiah and the people were rebuilding the wall, trouble arrived as they became surrounded by those who hated the Jews.

They all made plans to come and fight against Jerusalem and throw us into confusion. But we prayed to our God and guarded the city day and night to protect ourselves (Nehemiah 4:8-9).

What did Nehemiah do in this time of trouble?

"But we _____ to our God..." (verse 9).

How did God answer the peoples' prayers? God protected the people, and the wall was completed in only 52 days!

Jehoshaphat faced trouble. The kings of Judah and Israel went to war with the king of Aram. Jehoshaphat, king of Judah, found himself surrounded by the enemy.

So when the Aramean chariot commanders saw Jehoshaphat in his royal robes, they went after him. "There is the king of Israel!" they shouted. But Jehoshaphat called out, and the LORD saved him. God helped him by turning the attackers away from him (2 Chronicles 18:31).

What did God do when King Jehoshaphat cried out to the Lord?

"The LORD _____ him" and "God

_____ him..."

Queen Esther faced trouble. Esther's story is told in the book of the Bible named Esther. When this young queen was faced with the possibility that all her people, the Jews, would be killed, she made a request of her cousin Mordecai:

Go and gather together all the Jews of Susa and fast for me. Do not eat or drink for three days, night or day. My maids and I will do the same. And then, though it is against the law, I will go in to see the king. If I must die, I must die (Esther 4:16).

What statement shows Queen Esther's courage?

"If I _____ _____, I must _____."

After fasting for three days and nights, which was usually accompanied by prayer, Esther was ready to seek the king's help to save her people. In the end her people were saved from being killed!

Jesus spoke of trouble. Jesus spoke a parable about a widow who asked and asked and asked a judge to help her.

One day Jesus told his disciples a story to show that they should always pray and never give up (Luke 18:1).

What was Jesus' point? What was His message?

We "should _____ pray and

_____ _____ _____."

In Times of Need...Pray!

As you and I know, we run into trouble almost daily. We also know that Jesus tells us to bring our troubles to Him and He will help us handle them. But there is another area where we need God's help through prayer, and that is in times of personal need.

You probably have a long list of things you need to talk over with God. You have school problems, friend problems, and problems at home. You have doubts and worries about yourself. So what can you do?

The answer? In times of need...pray! You are to pray to God about your specific needs, and you can do that every day. *Underline* the words in the verses below that tell you *who* and *what* you are to pray for.

Pray for those who persecute you! (Matthew 5:44).

Give us today the food we need... (Matthew 6:11).

And don't let us yield to temptation, but rescue us from the evil one (Matthew 6:13).

Underline the words in the verse below that tell you what the apostle Paul asked others to pray about for him.

Pray for us, too, that God will give us many opportunities to speak about his mysterious plan concerning Christ (Colossians 4:3).

And don't forget to pray for your attitude. Pray for a joyful spirit, patience with others, and self-control. Galatians 5:22-23 is the perfect checklist for your attitude and actions. *Check* the three fruit of the Spirit you really need to pray about today.

__ love	__ patience	__ faithfulness
__ joy	__ kindness	__ gentleness
__ peace	__ goodness	__ self-control

I'm sure you realize that the list of your prayer needs can and should go on and on. So give your needs—each and every one of them—to your all-wise, all-powerful, and all-gracious God.

Are there some pressing needs today that you need to talk over with God—right here, right now? Make a list and offer them up to God in prayer.

_____

_____

_____

_____

_____

In Times of Helplessness...Pray!

There are times of trouble when you are completely helpless and cannot do anything but pray. For example,

- Your brother has a bike accident and is taken to the hospital. You can't do anything for your brother...but you can pray for his recovery.

- Your dad's job takes him away from home a lot. All you can do is pray for him and his safety and that he will return home soon.

I heard a story about a young boy named Danny who was saved from drowning by his brother John and carried home unconscious by his friends James and Thomas. A grateful father wanted to know exactly who had done what to help save his son.

John said, "I jumped into the water and pulled him out!"

James and Thomas said, "We carried Danny home!"

Poor little Mary, who was only three years old, burst into tears and said, "Daddy, I couldn't do anything at all, so I just prayed and prayed!"

Then her father gently said, "Mary, you deserve the most praise of all, for you did all you could, and God answered your prayers through John and James and Thomas."

In times of trouble...when you can't do anything at all...just pray and pray! During the tough times, when you don't know where else to go or what else to do, turn to God and pray.

Facing Your Troubles and Needs

Troubles and needs are facts of life. You may even be facing a difficult time in your life right now! But don't lose heart. God knows you and the issues you are facing. It's a fact of faith that you can deal with your problems through prayer. In the book of Jeremiah, we read about the many difficulties this faithful prophet faced. Even though he suffered, Jeremiah's faith and confidence in God is revealed in his prayers:

> But the LORD stands beside me like a great warrior.
> Before him my persecutors will stumble.
> They cannot defeat me (Jeremiah 20:11).

When troubles come your way—and they will—ask God to do what you cannot do. Don't lose hope. Don't stop trusting God. Instead, do as James 1:2 advises and see your troubles and personal needs in a positive way.

> ...when troubles of any kind come your way, consider it an opportunity for great joy.

In the verse above, *circle* the good thing you can gain through trials.

Believe it or not, God uses your troubles to give you greater strength, or endurance, as James goes on to say:

> ³ For you know that when your faith is tested, your endurance has a chance to grow.

⁴ *So let it grow, for when your endurance is fully developed, you will be perfect and complete, needing nothing* (James 1:3-4).

What happens when you endure your troubles and are patient and allow God to provide for your needs?

"...you will be _____

and _____, needing

_____" (verse 4).

After James explains that troubles produce endurance, he adds these words of encouragement for you:

Are any of you suffering hardships? You should pray. Are any of you happy? You should sing praises (James 5:13).

Praising God for His goodness and lovingkindness, and praying for strength during your troubles, gives you confidence in the Lord, "a mighty, awesome One" (Jeremiah 20:1 NKJV). Let the "awesome One" fight your battles. Trust in His ability to take care of you, and rejoice that He will judge and make things right. Don't lose heart—just bring your heart before God.

A PRAYER TO PRAY

Lord,

You have said in Your Word that I can come to You with my problems and You will help me handle them. Today I am bowing before You and asking You for help. Teach me through my problems. Thank You that I can come to You and trust You to show me the way to handle my problems. I praise You that You can do for me what I cannot do. Thank You.

Amen.

9

When It Comes to Worry... Pray!

Imagine it's the final inning of the last game of the baseball season. Your team has fought its way to the championship game. In the bottom of the ninth inning, the score is tied, the bases are loaded with two outs...and it all comes down to you! As the batter, you just need a walk or a hit to win the game and the championship. No pressure, right?

Wrong! Your stomach is tied in knots, and you are super worried! All the what-ifs in the world are whirling through your mind as you walk to the batter's box.

Even though world hunger is much more serious than the dilemma you face in a ball game, winning is still a big deal for you and your teammates!

So, what do you do when worry consumes you? One option is to muster up as much confidence as you can, go out on the field, and swing away. Or you can send up a quick prayer and ask God to calm your heart and give you His peace—and then go out there and swing away!

Which do you think would be the better choice?

Jesus Commands Us, "Do Not Worry!"

Let's see why Jesus, in His Sermon on the Mount, said we don't need to worry (Matthew 6:25-34). Obviously, the people of Jesus' day had a problem with worry too. As you read this portion of Jesus' sermon, look for and *circle* the three times Jesus tells the people not to worry.

²⁵ *That is why I tell you not to worry about everyday life—whether you have enough food and drink, or enough clothes to wear. Isn't life more than food, and your body more than clothing?*

²⁶ *Look at the birds. They don't plant or harvest or store food in barns, for your heavenly Father feeds them. And aren't you far more valuable to him than they are?*

²⁷ *Can all your worries add a single moment to your life?*

²⁸ *And why worry about your clothing? Look at the lilies of the field and how they grow. They don't work or make their clothing,*

²⁹ *yet Solomon in all his glory was not dressed as beautifully as they are.*

³⁰ *And if God cares so wonderfully for wildflowers that are here today and thrown into the fire tomorrow, he will certainly care for you. Why do you have so little faith?*

³¹ *So don't worry about these things, saying, "What will we eat? What will we drink? What will we wear?"*

³² *These things dominate the thoughts of unbelievers, but your heavenly Father already knows all your needs.*

³³ *Seek the Kingdom of God above all else, and live righteously, and he will give you everything you need.*

³⁴ *So don't worry about tomorrow, for tomorrow will bring its own worries. Today's trouble is enough for today.*

Wow, there are so many awesome truths in these verses! So pause and pray. Then read on to learn more about these truths.

In verse 25, what three everyday needs does Jesus say you are not to worry about?

_____

_____

_____

Also in verse 25, what does Jesus say is more important than food and clothing?

"Isn't _____ more than food, and your

_____ more than clothing?"

What animal does Jesus use in verse 26 as an illustration

of God's care? _____

To let you know how special you are to God, Jesus asks in verse 26,

"...aren't you _____ _____

_____ to him than they are?"

What flowers does Jesus use to illustrate that you don't need to worry about clothes (verses 28-30)?

_____ and _____

Jesus wraps up His message on trusting God:
"...if God cares so wonderfully for wildflowers...He will

certainly _____ _____ _____ "
(verse 30).

What sobering question does Jesus ask in verse 30?

"Why do you have _____ _____

_____ ?"

To sum up, Jesus tells us,

"...don't _____ _____

_____ _____..." (verse 31).

What two daily choices help you to focus on God and live for Him (verse 33)?

"_____ the _____ of

_____ above all else, and live _____..."

What does God promise as you seek and follow Him (verse 33)?

"...he will _____ you _____

you _____."

In verse 34, what does Jesus tell you *not* to do?

"...don't _____ about

_____..."

Are you understanding Jesus' message? He is saying that when you focus your attention on the things of the Lord, He will take care of all your needs...so you don't have to worry about anything!

The New Testament Tells Us Not to Worry

Jesus isn't the only one who tells us not to worry. The New Testament reminds us more than 300 times not to worry or be anxious. The apostle Paul gives us a better alternative in Philippians 4:6:

Don't worry about anything; instead, pray about everything. Tell God what you need, and thank him for all he has done.

Is there anything you are to worry about?

"Don't worry about _____..."

Rather than worry, what are you to do?

"...instead, _____ about _____."

What are you to tell God?

"...what you _____..."

What is the final thing we should do?

"...and _____ him for all he has done."

What is the result of praying rather than worrying?

Then you will experience God's peace, which exceeds anything we can understand. His peace will guard your hearts and minds as you live in Christ Jesus (Philippians 4:7).

"...you will experience God's _____..."

You cannot understand God's peace because it "exceeds anything we can _____."

As we have often said throughout this book, prayer is hard to understand. We talk to Someone we can't see...about things that are on our hearts...asking for help from this unseen Person. We don't understand how prayer works and how God can transform our worries into peace and calm.

It's like the prayer you whisper before you step in the batter's box. You can't explain it, but somehow God responds, and you feel at peace. You still may be a little nervous, but the worry is gone because you have turned everything over to God.

Now look at the second half of Philippians 4:7:

God's peace will "guard your hearts and minds," but to continue to experience that peace, you must live in

"_____ _____."

This brings us right back to what Jesus said in Matthew 6:33. To "live in Christ Jesus" means we are to seek His kingdom and live righteously—obeying God's Word. Our peace is directly related to how close we are to Jesus. Here's how it looks in an equation:

Living for yourself = worry.

Living for Jesus = peace.

You don't need to understand how prayer works. All you need to know is this:

Whatever is happening in your life,
whatever worry you may have,

God knows and loves you, and
He will take care of you.

Once again, you don't need to worry—about anything. You only need to know one thing:

Give all your worries and cares to God, for he cares about you (1 Peter 5:7).

Why do we know that we can give all our worries and cares over to God?

"...for he _____ about you."

Prayer Helps Us Not to Worry

In the beginning chapters of this book we talked about how difficult it is to start praying about anything and everything. We have super-busy lives, so it's easy to march forward making decisions, taking action, and saying things that later we would like to take back...but it's too late. We've goofed! That's one reason why prayer is important. It makes us wait...at least until our prayer is finished!

Well, here's some great news—another reason prayer is important. When you are faced with worries and difficult situations, through prayer you can talk to God and seek His heart and mind. Sometimes the things you are dealing with seem impossible. You wonder, "How am I going to get out of this?" or "How will I ever get through this?" In these impossible situations, when you don't know what to do, God gives you help when you pray—even when you don't know how to pray or what to pray for!

> *And the Holy Spirit helps us in our weakness. For example, we don't know what God wants us to pray for. But the Holy Spirit prays for us...*(Romans 8:26).

This is some really good news! When you don't know what to pray for, how to pray, or what words to use, who is there to help you?

"...the _____ _____ helps us..."

How does the Holy Spirit help?

"...the Holy Spirit _____ for us..."

It's awesome to know that you are not left on your own to deal with your problems and worries! Even when you don't know the right words to pray, the Holy Spirit does...and He prays with you and for you!

Why Worry?

The next time you are tempted to worry about anything or anyone, pick up your Bible and read Romans 8:38-39:

> *And I am convinced that nothing can ever separate us from God's love. Neither death nor life, neither angels nor demons, neither our fears for today nor our worries about*

tomorrow—not even the powers of hell can separate us from God's love. No power in the sky above or in the earth below—indeed, nothing in all creation will ever be able to separate us from the love of God that is revealed in Christ Jesus our Lord.

My young brother in Christ, God's love will never leave you, and His love will always be there to ease your worries, calm your heart, and assure you again and again of His love and care for you.

SEVEN REASONS NOT TO WORRY

Matthew 6

verse 25	The same God who created life in you can be trusted with the details of your life.
verse 26	Worrying about the future hampers your efforts for today.
verse 27	Worrying is more harmful than helpful.
verses 28-30	God does not ignore those who depend on Him.
verses 31-32	Worry shows a lack of faith and understanding of God.
verse 33	There are real challenges God wants us to pursue, and worrying keeps us from them.
verse 34	Living one day at a time keeps us from being consumed with worry.[3]

A PRAYER TO PRAY

Dear God,

I thank You for Your presence in my life. Nothing is impossible for You or unknown to You. Nothing happens in my life that You don't already know about. And nothing can separate me from Your love and care. So, Lord, now I see that I don't need to worry about anything! Thank You for the peace You give me. My heart's desire is to seek You daily and to live in a way that pleases You.

Amen.

10

When It Comes to the Future... Pray!

It's fun to read novels set in the future and sci-fi stories about time travel and Star Wars–type battles in far-off galaxies.

Wouldn't it be great to know the future? You could get up each day and know exactly what would happen. You would know what your family members were going to do when you showed up for breakfast. You would also know how the rest of your day, week, year, and life would go. You wouldn't need to trust God or to pray for His guidance. You wouldn't need the Bible, God's instructions for making decisions. You wouldn't even need your parents.

Maybe knowing the future isn't such a good idea after all! But seeking God's help as you move into your future *is* a good idea—a *very* good idea.

The future is the great unknown, and anything is possible, both good and evil. But the Bible says God is in control of all things. God tells us in Matthew 28:20, "And be sure of this: I am with you always, even to the end of the age."

No matter how uncertain the future seems, you can look forward to what's ahead because God will be there. God has done His part. Now you must do your part.

God's Plan for the Future

The Bible has a lot to say about the future and God's special plans for His people. Take a look at the future—*your* future.

God's plan will be for good. More than 2,500 years ago, the prophet Jeremiah sent a message from God to the exiled Jewish people. They had been taken to a land far away from their homes. They didn't know what was going to happen to them in the future, so God gave them this encouragement in Jeremiah 29:11:

> *"For I know the plans I have for you," says the* LORD. *"They are plans for good and not for disaster, to give you a future and a hope."*

What does this verse tell you about God's plan for your future?

"I know _____ _____ I _____

_____ _____...They are plans _____

_____ and not _____

_____, to give you a

_____ and a _____."

God's plan includes a home in heaven. Jesus told His disciples (which includes you and me) that He had plans for our future. What did these plans include? *Underline* the promises Jesus made in John 14:2-3:

> ² *My Father's house has many rooms; if that were not so, would I have told you that I am going there to prepare a place for you?*
>
> ³ *And if I go and prepare a place for you, I will come back and take you to be with me that you also may be where I am* (NIV).

Praying About Your Future

Knowing that the future is set, you can focus your life and prayers on the present. You can pray for God's leading today. Then tomorrow you can get up and begin praying again for another day of doing God's will and enjoying His blessings.

God's will is not a secret that is hidden from you. No, His will for your life is clearly described in the Bible. Your job as you grow into a man after God's own heart is to understand what God says about His desires for your future. Here are some things you should pray about as your future and God's will unfolds.

Pray about your obedience. As God's child, you are called to keep His commands. Obedience to God and His Word must be your number one prayer concern each day.

What happens to your prayers when you are disobedient and sinful?

If I regard wickedness in my heart,
The Lord will not hear... (Psalm 66:18 NASB).

"...the Lord will not _____..."

The best way to learn obedience to God and His commands is to start at home by obeying your parents. Let's look at Ephesians 6:1-3 again. As you read, *underline* God's commands.

¹ *Children, obey your parents because you belong to the Lord, for this is the right thing to do.*

² *"Honor your father and mother." This is the first commandment with a promise:*

³ *If you honor your father and mother, "things will go well for you, and you will have a long life on the earth."*

What happens when you honor your parents (verse 3)?

"...things will _____ _____ for you, and

you will _____ ___ _____

_____ on the earth."

God wants you to have a long and fruitful life. He wants things to go well for you. That is His ideal future for you. Do you want this kind of future? If so, complete this statement and then start praying daily for God to help you be obedient—not only to your parents but to all of God's commands in the Bible.

> With Your help, Lord, I will strive to honor and obey my parents, "for this is the right thing to do."

(Sign your name here) _____

(Write today's date here) _____

Pray about your spiritual growth. You will want to pray about this every day. Here's how it works:

> God's Word sets the boundaries of God's will. Prayer then helps you bring your will in line with God's will, which will be God's best future for you.

Underline what the following verses advise and command you to do about your spiritual growth.

> *Dear brothers and sisters, I close my letter with these last words: Be joyful. Grow to maturity* (2 Corinthians 13:11).

> *...[keep] asking God, the glorious Father of our Lord Jesus, to give you spiritual wisdom and insight so that you might grow in your knowledge of God* (Ephesians 1:17).

> *And may the Lord make your love for one another and for all people grow and overflow...*(1 Thessalonians 3:12).

May God give you more and more grace and peace as you grow in your knowledge of God and Jesus our Lord (2 Peter 1:2).

Pray about your purity. You and I live in a sinful world. Each day at school or in your neighborhood you are faced with kids who lie, cheat, use bad language, disrespect their parents, and are bullies. As one of God's knights and prayer warriors, you represent God to the world.

What is God asking of you? *Underline* the answer in the verse below.

But now you must be holy in everything you do, just as God who chose you is holy (1 Peter 1:15).

Holiness, or purity, probably isn't something you think about a lot, but as you grow older, you will be tempted to compromise your purity and act like the other kids. God knows this temptation is coming. What is His will for you in this area of purity?

God's will is for you to be holy, so stay away from all sexual sin (1 Thessalonians 4:3).

What is God's will for you? "...be _____..."

What is one way to be holy? "...stay away _____

_____ _____ _____."

Once again, prayer can help you be holy. You should pray each day to be a holy representative for God. *Underline* what God says He will do to help you with temptation and to keep you pure and holy.

> *...God is faithful. He will not allow the temptation to be more than you can stand. When you are tempted, he will show you a way out so that you can endure* (1 Corinthians 10:13).

Pray about your willingness to work. We are basically lazy people. It takes effort to get out of bed, get dressed, and go to school. It takes effort to do well in school, or to play a sport or musical instrument. As you learned in chapter 2, anything you want to do well will require time, training, dedication, and desire.

Your constant and daily prayers help you to be your best and do your best. It's easy to do just enough to get by, but that's not what God wants for you and your future. He wants the best *for* you and *from* you. So as you pray for diligence—in your chores around your home and your efforts in sports and other commitments—think and pray over this verse:

> *Work willingly at whatever you do, as though you were working for the Lord rather than for people* (Colossians 3:23).

Whom are you really working for?

"...for the _____ rather than for people."

As you honor God with your diligence, God will honor you with results, like better grades and better performance in all your efforts and activities.

Pray for wisdom. When you think of someone who has wisdom, do you imagine an old man, bent over and wearing a long gray beard and a pointed hat? He has a crooked staff in his hand, and he's giving out fatherly advice. Well, you can delete that picture from your mind because wisdom is not determined by your age or the color of your hair. Being wise means knowing and recognizing what is right and what is wrong.

Do you want wisdom? Here again is a familiar verse that reminds you of all you have to do:

If you need wisdom, ask our generous God, and he will give it to you. He will not rebuke you for asking (James 1:5).

What must you do to get wisdom? _____

_____

Where does God's gift of wisdom come from? *Underline* the source of wisdom.

For the LORD grants wisdom!
From his mouth come knowledge and understanding
(Proverbs 2:6).

Friend, decide now to dig into God's Word. When you do, you will become a wise young man who is able to make right choices.

As you lift up your heart to God in prayer and search through His Word, you will become more aware of God's direction and more open to following it. You will make wise choices. You will face each new day depending on God and looking to Him for guidance and direction. As you seek His direction, God will help you stay on the path of His will—His best and blessed future for you.

Show me the right path, O LORD;
point out the road for me to follow (Psalm 25:4).

A PRAYER TO PRAY

God,

You are my all-knowing Father. You know the beginning from the end and everything in between. I am so thankful You are in control of all things. I am Your child, and You hold my future in Your hands. You know my heart. You know the purpose You have for me. And you promise to finish Your work in my life. Help me, O Lord, not to be fearful of the future, but to fully trust You with my future. The desire of my heart is to love You and follow You to the finish line.

Amen.

Notes

1. Lila Empson, ed., *Checklist for Life for Teens* (Nashville, TN: Thomas Nelson, 2002), 81.

2. Jim George, *A Leader After God's Own Heart: 15 Ways to Lead with Strength* (Eugene, OR: Harvest House, 2012), 47.

3. *Life Application Study Bible* (Wheaton, IL: Tyndale House, 1998), 1338.

More Great Harvest House Books for Boys

by Jim George

A Boy After God's Own Heart

Jim George helps you understand why God is important in everything you do. He teaches what the Bible says about parents, making right choices, choosing good friends, taking school seriously, and following after God.

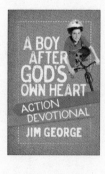

A Boy After God's Own Heart Action Devotional

If you're like most guys, you know how tough it can be to live for Jesus. It can be a challenge and sometimes a struggle, but anything worth going for is like that, right? God loves you and wants you to have a great life. All it takes is a minute or two each day to read these short chapters and learn how much He cares about you. You're super valuable to Him, and He has big dreams and huge plans for you that He wants you to discover.